THE TREADMILL
AND
THE ROPE

THE HISTORY OF A LIVERPOOL PRISON

TOD SLOAN

THE GALLERY PRESS
LEIGHTON BANASTRE, PARKGATE, SOUTH WIRRAL

ISBN 0 900389 30 3
Published by Gallery Press 1988
© D. (Tod) Sloan
Cover design by Didier Lemarchand
Printed by Scotprint (North West) Limited

CONTENTS

INTRODUCTION

Unlike most prisons throughout the World, which have survived for hundreds of years as permanent reminders to the human race that they must obey the rules of the controlling power, the Kirkdale House of Correction, to give it its official title, lasted less than a hundred years, during the nineteenth century, being built on open land in what is now the centre of Liverpool.

First occupied in 1819 and completed in 1821, it was appointed "The House of Correction for the Hundred of West Derby in the County of Lancashire".

Before 1819 prisoners of the Hundred were lodged in the Borough Gaol of Liverpool but this was found to be too small and inconvenient for administration. This problem being caused not only by the rapid growth of the prison population but the necessity to "collect for shipment" the thousands of people sentenced to be transported to "Lands across the Seas".

Increased pressure on penal establishments, combined with the work involved in attending to the execution of felons, was caused by the great unrest and riots in the Country and petty thieving for food that living conditions necessitated.

The governing political parties of the time, combined with the land and property owners in electing the judiciary, ensured that any threat to property, by either word or deed, was ruthlessly crushed.

It was the implementation of the "law" that filled the existing prisons and resulted in the building of The Kirkdale House of Correction. It was within this building, during its short existence, that the executive ensured that many of the greatest of British intellectual minds were imprisoned (which often also meant death), or transported to Australia.

At the end of the nineteenth century, the building was flattened to the ground and in an effort to remove its history many of the records applying to its existence were destroyed, misplaced or stored in archives far away from its original location in Liverpool.

It was with difficulty that these records were located, analysed and checked, to give an idea of the life and times of the prison itself and the people who, in some little way, either by choice, or without the option, were involved in its brief, but horrific history.

CHAPTER ONE

People may wish to locate the site of the building in relation to the centre of Liverpool, as it is today. It was located to the North of the City Centre in the district of Kirkdale. This area was considerably damaged by bombing during the 1939/45 war, leaving large tracts of land decimated. These have now been cleared and domestic dwellings erected. Accordingly, much of the area has changed dramatically. However, the area where the prison used to be remains exactly as it was when the prison was demolished.

In place of the prison building a recreation ground was laid-out with pathways, (remaining from the paths within the old prison building). This recreation ground remains, virtually unaltered to the present day, being used by people for walks, games and a playground for the children. During the 39/45 war it was used as a base from which a barrage balloon operated, which, at one time exploded causing considerable damage to the roofs and windows of local houses.

The "Kirkdale Rec", as it is known locally, is bounded by Garnett Avenue, Brock Street, North Dingle and Rumney Road West. Sessions Road, running from Fountains Road, formed a boulevard to what was the main approach to the building. The establishment consisted of two buildings, the House of Correction and the Sessions House, used for the administration of Justice.

On the 5th November 1821, the Sessions House was opened. This is where the General Quarter Sessions of the hundred of West Derby were held. It stood on the South front of the combined buildings, impressing the traveller with its grand portico, supported by six great Ionic columns. The Sessions Room was 70 feet long and 42 feet in width and had a suite of apartments adjoining, for the convenience of magistrates and barristers. This building remained for over fifty years after the demolition of the House of Correction, giving service to the local community as a public library, finally being demolished in the 1950s.

The House of Correction was one of the largest in the Kingdom, being constructed in circular form with two large wings. It was adapted to contain up to eight hundred prisoners, arranged in twenty-two classes. Great ingenuity went into the judicious classification of inmates to furnish them with employment suitable to their sex, crime, condition and circumstances.

A reputation for discipline and judicious management made Kirkdale internationally famous, and a precise model and a narrative explaining its regulations, management and organisation was sent, at his particular request, to the Emperor (Tsar) of Russia, for implementation within his own lands.

The building was erected at an initial expense of more than £80,000; occupying 28,648 square yards of land. The area was divided by partition walls into compartments which were under the observance of officers stationed in two circular lodges that commanded a view over all yards.

A Chapel stood in the centre and was connected to the lodges on each side by hanging bridges. The Governors house was on the North front and, at the time of its building, had a view that encompassed the entire entrance to the harbour of Liverpool and the East coast of Lancashire. The Chaplain resided in a picturesque cottage outside the prison walls, on the right of the approach to the Sessions House. Schools for Juvenile offenders and separate Hospitals for males and females were also enclosed within the walls. The whole construction being under the direction of Mr. Wright, an Architect from Manchester.

CHAPTER TWO

Authorisation for the commencement of construction of the prison was given by the Justices in 1818 after the Ormskirk and Wigan Sessions were transferred to Liverpool in 1817. This move was necessitated by the rapidly increasing population of Lancashire, indications of such a population growth being evident at the turn of the century. This increase reaching a peak between 1821 and 1841 when the population of Lancashire went from just over one million to 1,667,054, a two-thirds increase.

From 1808 to 1818 Britain was involved in many major wars, as well as a rising wave of civil unrest and little building of penal institutions took place. This is why in 1817, after the restructuring of the Assize responsibilities, there was an urgent requirement for the building of the Kirkdale House of Correction, especially in the hundred of West Derby, which enclosed, not only much of the development of the industrial revolution, but also had become home for many of the more recalcitrant workers of the County. To the Landowners and the Establishment these people, bearing in mind recent continental history, were a greater threat than all the overseas wars, requiring the application of the law, with all possible severity. Hence the necessity of Kirkdale Prison.

From the middle of the eighteenth century, Parliament proceeded to pass Acts relating to the administration of Prisons. These being instigated by a few reformers who were Members of the House. An example of some of the Acts are:

1759   Act making rules for the governing of prisons.

1773   Act ordering Justices to appoint Chaplains (which was largely ignored).

1774　Gaol Fever Bill (Regular Cleaning, Whitewashing, Ventilation, Appointment of Regular Doctor, Separate Sick Rooms).

1776　Hulk Act (Permitting the use of hulks for prisoners awaiting transportation or execution).

1779　Penitentiary Act (Penitentiaries under Council control).

1782　An Act requiring the separation of prisoners by sex and age, authorising workrooms and productive labour, and classification of prisoners according to their crime.

This output of Parliamentary Acts continued well into the nineteenth century, producing an overall description of "Prison Reform". These may well have reformed prison administration, but they did little to improve the life of the people most affected - the prisoners. Conditions remained harsh and warders brutal. Compassion was rare and the only moderator was wealth, but, in these Georgian years, for most people, life could be just as hard outside the prison walls.

Expenditure on prisons in the early nineteenth century, was a considerably higher proportion of the rates and taxes than in the twentieth century. Analysis of expenditure of the County of Lancashire and its hundred, between 1820 and 1842, shows the following proportions of expenditure:

Percentage Cost of Categories of Expenditure

County and Hundreds 1820-42

Item	%	Amount		
		£.	s.	d.
Prisons	38.7	763949	19	4
County & Private Lunatic Asylums	11.1	219432	17	7
Bridges	10.2	202023	0	11
Prosecutions	19.6	387444	4	10
Conducting Offenders to prison	4.3	85930	17	11
Passing Poor	2.4	47689	2	10

Coroners	2.4	47773	10	6
Law Expenses	1.3	24895	6	11
Riots	1.0	19308	16	6
Inspector of Weights & Measures	1.0	20652	14	6
County Constabulary	3.5	70008	15	0
Miscellaneous	4.3	84484	19	5
Total	100.0	1973594	6	3

Upon completion of the main buildings, the prison population was at its maximum for the first twenty years of its administration, as the following records indicate:-

Daily Average Population of Kirkdale Prison

1823	507	1833	574
1824	529	1834	573
1825	489	1835	627
1826	580	1836	615
1827	613	1837	337
1828	560	1838	368
1829	533	1839	315
1830	539	1840	344
1831	522	1841	317
1832	588	1842	494

In the 1840s there was a rebuilding programme, and in 1844, a sum of £8000 was spent on the building of a chapel. This expenditure caused quite a backlash from the ratepayers, moreso from the people confined within the prison. They were held under very arduous conditions, living on a per capita expenditure on food of five shillings per week, equal to 25p of decimal currency. People held in the Workhouse, which was only across the road, and was closely linked to the prison, were surviving on twenty four and a half pence per week. One can understand how they must have felt seeing such expenditure on a church.

Salaries about this time (1840), at Kirkdale, were:-

Governor	£400 per year
Chaplain	£300 per year
Surgeon	£180 per year
Matron	£100 per year.

Officers were very poorly paid, having to subsidise their salaries with "perks", as did everyone from the Governor down. The prison was staffed by incompetent men, as the rates of pay were, from the first, ridiculously low. The most incompetent and cruelest, staffed the Workhouse, usually having been transferred there from the prison, due to their excesses in behaviour, which proved to be too much even for the harsh regime of the correction service.

Councils throughout the Country were extremely frugal when it came to expenditure on prisons. With the service taking up such a high proportion of available rates, every endeavour was made to reduce costs. Cheesparing and petty measures, such as a diet of bread and gruel for the first fourteen days of every prisoner's confinement, had a knock on effect, reducing the ability to fight off illness thereby introducing conditions suitable for the spread of the plagues, which was a constant threat to life in those days. Salaries allocated for the payment of staff were so poor that only the most incompetent and illiterate people would take up the job, increasing the inhuman conditions which prisoners had to endure.

Committals by the Magistrates kept rising until 1834, when even these gentlemen were influenced by the deteriorating conditions in which convicts were confined. Being unable to improve conditions by obtaining a greater financial allocation to improve the situation, they developed a tendency to reduce the length of sentences, thereby alleviating the situation.

CHAPTER THREE

The ordinary life, work or punishment of prisoners in Kirkdale is a little difficult to separate as it was all of what, to us, would be a horrendous existence. Employment was found for all prisoners, men, women and children, classified as suitable to their particular crime, sex and circumstances. They were separated into classes and departments, each entirely distinct from each other.

Three departments were occupied by female prisoners, the remainder according to the particular type of crime of the offender. Amongst all departments would be a number of mental defectives or criminally lunatic people, of all ages. This type of prisoner, when not restrained in irons, caused trouble, not only for the staff, but also for the other inmates, by their irrational behaviour.

The Management of Kirkdale however, were proud of the "great vigilance that is exercised in proportioning the duration of the labour to the criminality of the culprit". Hardened and serious offenders worked for six hours a day, while the less hardened escaped with a punishment of only four hours daily labour.

This work covered many functions but, the main one, which Kirkdale became famous for, was on its "tread-wheel". The description, tread-wheel, being its official designation but it was at Kirkdale that the expression "tread-mill" became a common description, due to its main function of grinding flour.

The tread-mill at Kirkdale was the largest in the Kingdom, requiring the propulsion of the continuous labour of 130 prisoners at any one time, throughout twenty four hours a day. This tread-mill, officially described as Cubitts Tread-wheel, had been unknown until the 1820s, but became popular when the Judiciary realised they had a free source of power in the prisoners. Its introduction into other prisons followed after its success had been demonstrated at Kirkdale.

Although the Kirkdale tread-mill was used to grind wheat into flour, other prisons used theirs to drive looms. For example, the tread-mill at Preston Prison was used for weaving, with shirt making, for sale by the Magistrates, being the end product.

In 1825, Mr. W. Horner, the Chaplain of Kirkdale Prison wrote:

"The treadmill which is found to be very beneficial to the health of the women is proportionately injurious to their moral improvement. It seems to create a carelessness and indifference to reproof and punishment which was never observed before. Its effect on the men is of the same kind, but not perhaps to the same degree. Without imputing bad feelings to them, this may perhaps be accounted for by the spirits resulting from moderate exercise contrasted with the despondency attending their former continued, unvaried, sedentary occupations".

If there were too many prisoners available to fill all the places on the tread-mill, "shot-drill" was used instead. This was a type of work/punishment that had been used before the innovation of the tread-mill, requiring each prisoner having a stack of cannon balls at one side of the yard which had to be carried across to the other side and stacked into a pyramid, 91 in a stack. Upon completion of this task, he then had to repeat the performance, back again, carrying on until he had satisfied his quota, before being allowed to rest.

Naturally, in addition to the wheel and the shot, prisoners were used for other work. Labour of the second class consisted of mat and rug making, weaving handkerchiefs, picking oakum, or any other jobs the Magistrates and Governor would consider to be financially viable to themselves.

Internal punishments for misdemeanours, other than additional time on the wheel or the shot, were Whipping, Ironing (Shackling with ball and chains or to complete immobility) and/or solitary confinement with dietary restrictions.

Sickness and death was the constant cell mate of all prisoners. Throughout its history, Kirkdale had the highest death rate of any prison in the British Isles. Several prisons in Lancashire had a higher incidence of sickness but none, had a death rate as high as Kirkdale. Lancaster Castle had a high rate of death, but a very low incidence of sickness, while Preston Prison, although having a high sickness rate, had very few prisoners die. A comparison of these three prisons, over a ten year period, just after Kirkdale had been built shows this variance. However, it must be remembered that these figures do not include felons executed, or an unknown number of children who died within the prison.

Year	Lancaster		Preston		Kirkdale	
	Sick	Died	Sick	Died	Sick	Died
1823	17	0	15	1	33	8
1824	43	1	—	—	133	4
1825	54	3	509	0	143	15
1826	105	10	556	3	254	6
1827	82	11	520	3	156	13
1828	99	12	480	0	127	11
1829	66	18	416	1	138	5
1830	57	6	463	3	131	7
1831	63	11	557	0	137	6
1832	90	10	533	2	57	35

Tuberculosis was the main cause of death in Kirkdale although, in the mid eighteen-forties, Scurvy became a problem, the Kirkdale Prison Surgeon recording that it had never been known before in the prison. Venereal Disease also caused many deaths. Typhus took its toll in line with the plagues that periodically swept over Liverpool during this era and it was after one such epidemic in 1832 that records of sickness were not kept for several years.

Physical deformity and hereditary ailments, combined with the disabilities of the wounded from many wars, did not require their segregation from fit prisoners. It was quite normal to observe limbless prisoners, mixing with the blind. Many suffered from Rickets and others with T.B. Others with Downes Syndrome (Mongoloid, in those days) mixing with some who had facial deformities resulting from the ravages of Syphilis, wearing triangular patches where their nose used to be.

Afflictions were never allowed as extenuating circumstances against sentence, and their commitment to prison would not only have increased their own suffering, but added to the torment of those inmates of previously good health.

An examination of the type of prisoner and the respective ways in which they passed their "recreation time" requires an analysis of the types of crime for which they were convicted. As an example, take the "Calendar of all the Prisoners in Kirkdale", for the 28th April 1823. (Issued by the Governor, Thomas Amos.)

Offence	Male Convicts	Female Convicts
Felony	188	102
Bastardy	18	11
Burglary	1	0
Uttering Base Coin	6	4
Keeping a Private Still	9	2
Assault	13	1
Neglect of Family	3	0
Neglect of Work	10	1
Vagrancy	17	1
Poaching	2	0
Hawking without Licence	1	0
Disorderly	0	13
Desertion	1	0
Misdemeanor	24	2
Total	293	137

Of those convicted of felony, 8 males and 18 females were awaiting transportation to the penal colonies in Australia.

Twenty four males had been whipped twice, as part of their sentence.

Most of those serving sentences for Bastardy were imprisoned for three months, unless sums of between £1 and £6 were paid to the Overseers of various Workhouses in the region towards the maintenance of their children. Serving the sentence, however, did not clear these debts and unless ultimately paid could result in ever increasing and recurring sentences of imprisonment.

The average age of all prisoners was twenty seven years, eleven per cent of whom were under the age of fourteen, quite a few being under ten years of age.

Many prisoners were illiterate and a report in 1844, intending to demonstrate the degree of ignorance, produced the following figures:-

Unable to name the months
    of the year   50 percent
Ignorant of the name of
    the reigning Sovereign   39 per cent

Ignorant of the words "virtue", "vice", and "righteousness"	43 percent
Unable to count to a hundred	15 percent

Less serious offenders in Kirkdale would often be found practising their respective trades, Cobblers working on boots, Tailors on clothing, etc. Groups were permitted to gather to converse, usually on political theories and the abilities of notable personages. Artists were allowed to record prison scenes, which could be published upon release.

Prisoners were permitted to smoke at certain times, having purchased their requirements from the Gaolers. Drinking was encouraged as, once again, alcoholic drink could be purchased from Gaolers who, in prison terms, "Held the Tap", this being the prize "perk" for these officials. Drunkenness was a constant cause of trouble, both with prisoners and staff. The Governor on many occasions having to order restraint in Irons for his own staff.

Lunatics, however, remained a constant conundrum for both gaolers and prisoners alike. They were very common in Houses of Correction, which served as a convenient dumping ground for problem cases which, for one reason or another, were not suited for more specialised institutions. William John Williams wrote in 1839, "Every tour of inspection affords me fresh examples of the inconvenience of retaining in prisons individuals acquitted of crime on the grounds of insanity, but ordered to be detained during pleasure. They can be set no labour or employment; are often restless and uncertain in temper; dissatisfied with their situation and unsafe, even to be trusted with the execution of the most menial of office". Seven of the thirteen visits made by the Visiting Justices of Kirkdale to the prison in 1844-45 were to see insane prisoners.

Prisoners could become insane after committal. A condition which was not improved by the common punishment for their misbehaviour by confinement in the refactory cells and keeping in Irons. The gaolers certainly had no idea of psychology, usually responding to madness by slamming the doors and trying to forget the presence of this trouble they could do nothing about. They offered no treatment, exercise or solace and very little food, in conditions beyond normal understanding.

One of the penalties which all prisoners had to endure was noise. Day and night, the screams of the insane, the moans of the sick and dying, with the cries of those under punishment, would combine with what could be called normal sounds of prison life.

Another problem was that of smell. Cess pit sewerage combining with the smell from several hundred unwashed bodies, added to the constant odours arising from human gasses caused by the diet which prisoners lived on. All aggravated by the overpowering odour of gangrene and corrupting bodies.

Although prisoners had to suffer with most of their natural senses, there was one that carried them through their ordeal. Their Sense of Humour usually helped them in the most horrendous situations. The majority of inmates were from Liverpool and the surrounding area and for some biological reason caused by the cross breeding of the various races who formed a life together, Irish, Scots, Welsh and English with a little bit of many other Nations, they developed a type of character which is unique in this World. No matter how perilous or traumatic the conditions, someone would always see the humour of the situation, and everyone else joined in the laughter. Accordingly, Kirkdale Prison, no matter how grim in real life, developed a reputation for having prisoners that were incorrigible and the institution ultimately became known for its idle and convivial atmosphere.

Executions, punishments, plagues and pestilence - someone, somewhere in the prison, would find it funny, which helped everyone to get through another day. This ability to find humour in the most arduous of situations was not just restricted to the prison. The crowds which gathered outside the prison for the entertainment of a public execution, were known for their repartee. It continues in the area, even in the twentieth century, as may be witnessed by the humour of the crowds who gather at Liverpool football matches. Quite a few of the felons executed at Kirkdale are recorded as having left this life with a smile on their face, having cracked a joke with the executioner. You have got to have a sense of humour to survive in Liverpool, and a better one to die there.

CHAPTER FOUR

Prisoners and their crimes must be considered to understand the necessity of Kirkdale Prison. In addition to those due for execution and the numbers being collected ready for transportation, there were quite clearly defined types of so-called criminals.

Felons were kept in separate wings, according to the severity of their sentence. Those sentenced to transportation (usually for seven years) were, in retrospect, "lucky". To sentence a man to seven years in prison, under such conditions, was tantamount to a sentence of slow death. He, or she, would almost certainly die of one of the prevailing diseases, having been weakened by the conditions under which they were confined.

There was no such thing as a "Top Security Wing", which is a relatively modern innovation. Prisoners who, in the twentieth century, would have been put into this classification, did not exist ... they would have been executed, having been sentenced under laws carrying more draconian penalties than laws which exist today. Special wings, however, were hardly necessary as the whole place was virtually escape proof, with horrendous punishment and retribution for those who would try.

Many were imprisoned for what could be called minor crimes and misdemeanours. A lot were associated with the theft of food or coal. No one steals such things unless they are driven to it by prevailing conditions, so one could say that many were imprisoned for trying to maintain their families. Once incarcerated, they knew their children would be living under even harder conditions than themselves ... usually, just across the road in the Workhouse. What torment of mind these prisoners must have suffered.

Others were in prison for their political and humanist ideals, and there were many strongly held views and radical ideas within the population of the Liverpool and West Lancashire areas. People were not afraid to speak their minds, regardless of the ulimate consequences. The area was regarded by the landowners and Judiciary as a hotbed of rebellion and traitorous activities. Putting them away in Kirkdale and other prisons, on any charge possible, was one way of keeping the discontent under control and, with the Transportation of Felons Act, the opportunity of being able to get rid of many outspoken people, on relatively minor charges was used at every Sessions.

In the first half of the Nineteenth Century, the number of prisoners kept increasing as Parliament declared more and more acts to be felonies. Economic uncertainty increased the number of imprisoned debtors and the Government, preoccupied with political upheaval, failed to take any measures to release them. Social upheaval during the early part of the Industrial Revolution also caused a real increase in the numbers of so called crimes being committed. Many prisoners were held for years on one long term remand after another while awaiting the decision of the Crown.

Between 1810 and 1840 there was over four hundred incidents in Liverpool and West Lancashire which were regarded as uprisings and where the Riot Act was read. Ormskirk, Burscough, Upholland, Wigan, Warrington, Culcheth, Windle, Altcar, Widnes and Newton, as well as Liverpool were all areas where the population rioted. The whole of Lancashire was in turmoil. In 1812 there were the Lancashire Luddite disturbances, eight were executed, seventeen transported and seven imprisoned. Also in 1812, there were other disturbances, known as the Luddite 38s. The accused were acquitted, but they were penalised later on other charges. In 1817 there was the incident known as the Blanketeer rising for which 29 were imprisoned and, on the 16th August 1819, there occurred what became known as the Peterloo Massacre in Manchester. Many including Hunt and Johnson were imprisoned. In 1830, the winners of an election in Preston, this being one of the few towns where every man had a vote, were called the Hintide Mob and charged with Seditious Conspiracy by the Landowners and Judiciary This was a relatively minor charge carrying up to a years imprisonment with Riotous Assembly being a far more serious charge. Kirkdale Prison held eighty prisoners charged with Riotous Assembly.

In 1834 the Tolpuddle Martyrs were tried and transported, which became a cause celebre. But before this, many hundreds of men and women served time in Kirkdale for activities associated with free speech and the democratic rights and freedoms of workers. Placing them in confinement together, the Authorities allowed the exchange of ideas and development of policies. Although the Trades Union movement gathered momentum at a later date, it was at this time, and in Kirkdale Prison, that the foundations were laid.

To understand the conditions influencing so much civil unrest in Liverpool and Lancashire, one must appreciate the deteriorating quality of life for the working classes, compared to the increasing affluence of the aristocracy and middle classes. They improved their own conditions, in line with Britain's colonialisation and expansion programme overseas. None of these benefits came to the ordinary people, especially for those from Liverpool and West Lancashire, for whom the desire to eat supplied a ready supply of cheap labour, much of which was surplus to requirement, as the effect of industrialisation reduced the need for manual labour.

The commencement of building of Kirkdale Prison was during the reign of George IV, (1820-1830) who was best known for his extravagances and moral laxity. He was followed by William IV (1830-1837), and finally, Victoria (1837-1901). During this period, covering the reign of three monarchs, Britain was controlled by three "major" Prime Ministers, Sir Robert Peel, Conservative (1841-46), William Gladstone, Liberal (1868-74), who endeavoured to reform the legal and education systems of the County, and Benjamin Disraeli, Conservative, who was in power in 1868 and again in the period 1874-80.

Records of the life style of ordinary people during this period are available, but must be assessed allowing for any bias. Those who were not within the prevailing system were never in a position to instigate official returns, and most authors were from the privileged classes. Very little "working class" reporting being available to the public. However, there was one outstanding exception to these limitations ... Charles Dickens. By training and occupation he was a reporter, with an eye for facts and detail. He is known for his great stories which, although fiction, were in most cases based on fact, and his description of social conditions is certainly true. He probably did more than any other living person of the time to expose the terrible conditions under which man was expected to live.

If one examines the dates at which he wrote many of his most famous stories, one can appreciate he was describing the conditions under which people survived during the existence of Kirkdale prison:-

21

Pickwick Papers	1836-37
Oliver Twist	1837-38
Nicholas Nickleby	1838-39
The Old Curiosity Shop	1840-41
Martin Chuzzlewick	1843-44
David Copperfield	1849-50
Hard Times	1852-53
Our Mutual Friend	1864-65
Great Expectations	1880-81

The majority of people associate "the world of Dickens" with the London area, especially people from the North West Counties. Few realise that conditions in Liverpool were considerably worse than the most harrowing of Dickens's stories.

For example, in the eighteen-sixties, in Liverpool alone, (remembering it was only a small town in those days), upwards of 5000 people, including children, were in the workhouses of the area at any one time. During this same period, in the same town, the average number of people residing, per house, was fifteen, with many houses towards the centre of the town providing shelter for over fifty people each night, sleeping in every available space, crushed in under conditions which would not be acceptable for wild animals today. Unimaginable poverty existed which was associated with the spread of terrible diseases and afflictions.

Amidst all the suffering, people were constantly being reminded of their place in society by, not only the sight of Kirkdale Prison, but the stories which were told about what went on within it's walls.

An article in the local newspaper describes the scene as follows:-

"The grim walls of the County Gaol frowned down upon the hollow of Kirk Dale and viewed from any point Westward, were repulsive enough to strike terror into the hearts of the cattle which browsed on the scanty herbage of the dale."

It is certain that if one was a felon, being held in Kirkdale awaiting transportation, one must have actually looked forward to the voyage, even with all its hazards.

CHAPTER FIVE

After its completion, Kirkdale Prison was used, until 1834, as a staging post for the collection of prisoners sentenced to transportation. People had no idea what the process of transportation involved in its early stages. Such information was restricted and not published for public consumption.

The use of transportation originated in the sixteenth century. An Act for the "Punishment of Rogues, Vagabonds and Sturdy Beggers ... To be banished out of this Realm and all other Dominions thereof", was introduced into English Law in 1597. Further acts relating to transportation were passed in 1664, 1666, and 1718. Transportation was classified as a punishment second only to the death penalty in severity and for almost two hundred years, felons were shipped to Virginia, Jamaica and Barbados.

Due to the War of American Independence in 1776, transportation was halted and those that would have been sentenced to banishment were used for hard labour in England under an Act of 1776. After a gap of ten years it was decided that these prisoners could be better employed in Britain's new colonies in the southern hemisphere. Accordingly, in 1784, an Act was passed ordering that transportation be resumed on a regular basis. This was mainly to reduce the pressure on existing gaols and hulks.

The first fleet of ships carrying convicts to Australia, left England on 13th May 1787, arriving in Botany Bay on 20th January 1788. The fleet consisted of six vessels, plus three storeships and two Royal Navy escort ships. They carried officials, free settlers and seamen, but by far the largest group was of 788 convicts. Free Settlers were those who of their own free will, went to Australia to make a home for themselves, encouraged by land grants and other concessions.

In the early 1800's cost of transportation worked out at One Pound, One Shilling and Seven Pence per prisoner. Poor food on board, consisting of gruel, bread, ships biscuits and salt beef, (all of which deteriorated in quality throughout the voyage), resulted in dysentry, scurvy, and ultimately death.

Most prison ships sailed via Tenerife, Cape Verde and the Cape of Good Hope, but often, through lack of fresh water were forced to divert to Rio de Janeiro in Brazil.

When people were sentenced, there was no possible way they could be sent overseas immediately. Prisoners had to be collected into economical loads for the convict ships, and in many cases into convoy loads. This would involve convicts being confined to prisons or hulks for up to two years, before transportation and the commencement of their actual sentence. This prolonged confinement, especially in Kirkdale, so debilitated the prisoners that their chance of surviving a voyage, of up to eight months, under convict ship conditions, was considerably reduced. In fact almost half of prisoners transported, via Kirkdale, died on the journey.

In the twentieth century, a myth has developed that Australia was originally populated by criminals transported from the British Isles. Analysis of the records would indicate that these people, far from being criminals in the recognised understanding of the word, were considerably better types than those who ordered their transportation. Many were considerate, gentle people, forced by circumstances to maintain their dependents under horrific social conditions. Others were what would now be called British Dissidents and Humanists. Criminals, in a moral sense, they certainly were not ... an appreciation of the severity of British Law at the time would show that any real criminal would have been executed, without exception.

History has shown that the transportation programme was Britain's loss and Australia's gain. One has only to examine the development of the Australian continent to appreciate the moral fibre of its original settlers and to accept that only "the best of British" were transported. The original stock would not only have been of a superior moral standard but the trials and tribulations of the imprisonment and voyage would have ensured that only the fittest and strongest, in mind and body survived. This superior blood line can be seen in their descendents of the present day.

After completion of sentence, a prisoner could return home to Britain ... if they could afford the fare. However, after a period of good behaviour he, or she, could be granted a conditional pardon which allowed them complete freedom in Australia. But they could not return to Britain within the period of the original sentence. To do so meant death. Many convicts, after being granted a conditional pardon, took up minor positions in the Government Service. The prisons in Australia, in particular, being staffed by ex-convicts. A "Ticket of Leave" allowed a prisoner to leave the Government Department "for his own Private Advantage". Absolute Pardons returned a convict to complete freedom, but were rarely granted. Relatives and dependents of transported felons constantly offered petitions to the Home Secretary requesting their freedom. These were usually supported by local Churchmen or other Dignitaries, aware of the suffering of the families left behind. They were rarely successful.

Transportation was ended in 1868, to be superceded by Penal Servitude.

Between 1788 and 1868, 162,000 men and women were transported. But there were still over 100 crimes for which the death penalty could be imposed. Transportation, at least, gave them some sort of chance.

To appreciate the types of crime for which people were transported, let us examine the "Kirkdale Calendar of Prisoners". Those sentenced to transportation are listed and the date of conviction should be noted in relation to the date of this record, 28th April 1823.

Summary of felons sentenced to be transported, held in the County House of Correction, Kirkdale, 28th April 1823.

Names	Sex	Date/Place & Sentence
Mary Chamley	F	7 May 1821. Liverpool Sessions. Transported 7 years.
Mary Davies	F	21 May 1821. County Sessions. Transported 7 years.
Alice Turtle	F	23 July 1821. Liverpool Borough Sessions. Transported 7 years.
Ann Robinson	F	30 July 1821. County Sessions. Transported 7 years.

Eliza Finnigan	F	4 February 1822. County Sessions. Transported 7 years.
Elizabeth Winrow	F	6 May 1822. County Sessions. Transported 7 years.
Ann Stannaway	F	6 May 1822.
Marg. Stringfellow	F	County Sessions. Transported 14 years.
Ann Simms	F	15 August 1822. County Sessions. Transported 7 years.
Margaret Graham	F	21 October 1822.
Mary Duffey	F	Liverpool Borough Sessions.
Elizabeth Maddox	F	Transported 7 years.
Mary Gleaves	F	
Elizabeth Jones	F	
Margt. Ferguson	F	
Elizabeth Stopford	F	
Mary Lynch	F	20 January 1823. Liverpool Borough Sessions. Transported 7 years
Ann Connor	F	3 February 1823. County Sessions. Transported 7 years.
Robert Nicholson	M	5 November 1821
James Burke	M	County Sessions. Transported 7 years.
Samuel Dunbabin	M	20 January 1823. Liverpool Borough Sessions Transported 7 years.
Edward Moore	M	3 February 1823.
Moses James	M	County Sessions. Transported 7 years.
Edward Jones	M	14 April 1823.

| John Brown | M | Liverpool Borough Sessions. Transported 7 years. |

Examination of the Court Records of the proceedings in a sample of these cases gives the following information:-

| Mary Davies | Sentenced with Cath. Swinburn at Kirkdale, to transportation for stealing 10 yards of cotton. |

| Ann Robinson | Sentenced with Catherine Wilson at Kirkdale, to transportation for stealing 2 pieces of calico. |

| Eliza Finnigan | Sentenced at Kirkdale, to transportation for stealing 5 handkerchiefs. |

| Elizabeth Winrow | Sentenced at Ormskirk, to transportation for stealing £2. 10s and a watch. |

| Ann Stannaway Marg. Stringfellow | Sentenced at Kirkdale, to 14 years transportation for receiving 1000 yards of cloth. (David Davies, Robert Filkin & Samuel Eaton, who were convicted of stealing the cloth were sentenced to 7 years transportation). |

| Ann Simms | Sentenced at Kirkdale, to transportation for stealing 30 yards crepe. |

| Ann Connor | Sentenced at Kirkdale, to transportation for stealing one coat. |

| Margaret Graham Mary Duffey Elizabeth Maddox Mary Gleaves Elizabeth Jones Margt. Ferguson Elizabeth Stopford | All were sentenced at Kirkdale, to transportation for "picking pockets". In most cases the male "victims" were not wearing their trousers at the time.
Their trial is notable in that they were all isolated cases, but were tried together.
Mary Gleaves, upon sentence, managed to throw a rock at the Justices, with the comment of "If I'm going to go, I may as well go for something decent".
There is no record of her having her sentence increased. |

Robert Nicholson	Sentenced at Kirkdale, to transportation for stealing one ham.
Edward Moore	Sentenced at Kirkdale, to transportation for stealing one pair of stockings.
Moses James	Sentenced at Kirkdale, to transportation for stealing one shirt.

It should be noted the severity with which Justices dealt with women. There was also a distinct touch of a lottery as to when you went for trial. Over the five year period 1818 to 1822, (and with similar pattern thereafter), 23 per cent of all convictions in the Autumn Assizes were transported, but only 10 per cent if they were convicted in the Spring Assizes.

Also, during this same period, 69 per cent of all women convicted of a felony were transported. Of 177 people sentenced to transportation, 128 of them were women.

CHAPTER SIX

Liverpool has always appreciated its entertainers. Stars of stage and sport, receive adulation from the population, providing their performance has been good and their act skilful. No performers, however, received more respect, when they visited the area, than the men who called at Kirkdale Prison on a regular basis. These were the Public Executioners, who had cause to attend to their duties many times during the nineteenth century, when a long list of crimes was punishable by death.

From the beginning, Kirkdale prison was very busy in the execution business and people used to look out for the executioners, who became well known to the population, as they arrived in Liverpool by train for their appointments.

The most famous of these executioners were Calcraft and Marwood, but there were others who stood in as substitutes.

Calcraft was one of the longest serving, working until he was seventy three years of age. During his long career, he attended to many thousands of executions, including several mass hangings at Tyburn. The most he topped at Kirkdale however was four at one time in 1863. His technique was poor and the condemned man usually died of strangulation. His last execution at Kirkdale was in 1873, when he made such a mess of the job the Officials refused to use him again.

Howard, the York Executioner, was used at odd times during this period when Calcraft was indisposed. Being of a nervous disposition, he also made quite a mess of anything he did.

Mr Anderson took over for a short period after Calcraft retired. This was a nom-de-plume and his real name was Evans, a sheep farmer from North Wales. Although an "amateur", he looked and dressed the part, working quite efficiently.

Marwood took over in 1875, attending to executions for a period of over seven years. He did more for the art of execution than anyone before or since. Developing the long drop, causing death by dislocation of the spinal vertebrae, and by using skilled assistants, speeded up the whole operation.

Only once did the last three executioners ever meet – in 1875, in the Sessions Hotel in Kirkdale, where the techniques of the long drop were discussed, later to be put into effect by Marwood.

This method of execution was adopted as standard by the Home Office and was included in the techniques taught at a "school" for executioners and their assistants, held at Wormwood Scrubs Prison under the auspices of the Home Office, until the 1960s.

Until 1868 executions were public, the last one in England being of Michael Barrett on the 26th May 1868, a Fennian, hanged at Newgate.

For the first forty seven years of its existence Kirkdale Prison provided many public hangings for the entertainment of the people. Afterwards they were held within the confines of the prison.

At all executions throughout this period representatives of the Press were present, being close to the gallows as witnesses. Accordingly, most executions are well documented in newspaper reports and give a good idea of the atmosphere at the time. In order to illustrate the difference between executions held in public and within the prison and the different methods of executioners working at Kirkdale, here are a sample of newspaper reports covering the work of all the above mentioned men. (The grammar of the period is retained in these reports).

Execution of Gleeson Wilson, 1849. Executioner – Howard

John Gleeson Wilson, alias Maurice Wilson, was accused that in the spring of 1849 he entered the house of Captain Henricksen in Leveson Street, Great George Street and deliberately butchered Mrs Henricksen, her two boys, aged respectively three and five years, together with the servant Mary Parr. After an investigation Wilson was apprehended by the Police and following a preliminary hearing before the stipendary magistrate, he was committed to take his trial at the Assizes.

August 23rd, 1849, the day of the trial, would be for years after remembered and talked about by those who were present. Each day they thought might be the day appointed for the trial, and not for any money would those who had squeezed their way in have given up their chance of seeing the sight.

At last the patience of those who found their way into the Sessions House on Thursday, August 23rd, was rewarded. And yet, when Mr Justice Patteson took his seat, things did not look at all promising for sightseers. For his Lordship proceeded to deal with some ordinary cases, and it was not until one o'clock that Gleeson Wilson was placed in the dock, and indicted for the murder of Mary Parr.

As Mr. Serjeant Wilkins, who conducted the prosecution, rose to open his case, a stillness as of death fell upon the court and every eye was turned upon the prisoner.

Although far from prepossessing, Wilson was not altogether a bad looking man. Of medium height, his slender build barely credited him with the 26 years he was said to have passed in this mortal life. His wavy brown hair was carefully parted on the right side, and with an air of jaunty indifference he listened as the serjeant fitted in link after link of the damning chain of evidence, his head, inclining slightly to the left, sent a mass of hair almost to his coat collar.

Although Wilson's counsel, Messrs Pollock and Brett, made a gallant fight for their client, the weight of evidence was too strong.

The judge summed up briefly but to the point, and the jury, after turning round in their box for a bare three minutes, returned a verdict of guilty.

Several times was Justice Patteson interrupted while passing sentence of death on the prisoner who, with tears in his eyes, vehemently protested his innocence. But his lordship at length went steadily on despite the convict's interpolations, and his calm and measured tones as he consigned Wilson to a well-merited doom quietened, if they did not entirely quell, the murderer's frantic appeals for mercy.

As the concluding sentence fell from the judge's lips there was some applause in court which was, however, immediately repressed. But the crowd outside cheered vehemently.

Considerable uncertainty prevailed in the public mind as to the date when the execution would be carried out. A report to the effect that it would take place on Saturday, September 8th, was countenanced by the authorities; and on that day thousands of people assembled in the fields commanding a view of the north-west angle of Kirkdale Gaol, and waited patiently until the afternoon was far advanced.

Deprived of the imposing spectacle they had come to see, the crowd went in very extensively for rough horse-play. The cornermen of the period, who had mustered in strong force, organised little excursions in the neighbourhood of any respectably-dressed persons, and robbed them with impunity of their watches and money. In one instance a party of six made a little mistake in attempting to relieve the ex-champion of England of his watch and chain. But a series of terrific right-handers stretched five of the roughs senseless on the ground, while the sixth made his escape by wriggling deftly through the crowd.

As a specimen of the prevailing taste of the time, one case may be cited.

On the previous afternoon (Friday), a gentleman met an old man and woman, both of whom had considerably passed the allotted term of life, toiling painfully along the dusty road leading from one of the outlying districts to Kirkdale. They stopped to inquire the way to the prison and, in reply to a remark told him they were going to see the execution. "But," remonstrated the gentleman, "You are a week too soon." "We don't mind that, sir." replied the quasi-octogenarian. "We shall be in lots of time; we were too late last hanging we came to, and we can wait."

In the week ending September 15th it became pretty generally known that on the Saturday Gleeson Wilson would offer up the only expiation of his crime.

Early on the Friday morning carts were drawn into good positions near the gaol walls. But their owners, who anticipated a rich harvest from visitors who would be willing to pay a good price for standing room on the vehicles were disappointed for Mr. Gibbs, the governor of the prison, promptly ordered all the conveyances away, enforcing his command by the aid of the police, who were aleady beginning to take up positions on the ground.

As the afternoon sunlight began to fade away into a subdued golden glow, to be again succeeded by the deepening haze of twilight, the people began to arrive in two's amd three's, and in dozens, and to make preparations for spending the eighteen hours or so that would intervene before the execution would take place. And what a gathering it was; thieves and prostitutes plied their calling unchecked and unhampered. The scourings of Vauxhall Road and Scotland Road, and the courts and alleys of the South-end vomited forth their unwashed denizens by the hundred. Venders of every description of edible and potable yelled forth the price and description of their wares, and when the night had fallen the camp fires lighted here and there showed in their pitiful gleams a veritable pandemonium in which the dusky forms, flittering here and there, would well have passed for the denizens of another world.

The foundation of the scaffold, the construction of which was eagerly watched, was formed by two beams about four yards apart, projecting from holes in the prison walls. Two upright and one cross beam, from which depended a short iron chain with a link to which the hook of the rope would be attached, formed the "fruitless tree". Attached to the projecting beam was a kind of box with folding lids, the outside covered with black cloth.

On top of this box stands the convict, the greater part of his body being exposed to view as he steps upon the drop. About breast high an iron rod passes round the scaffold, and when the bolt is drawn the top of the box falls apart and the criminal remains suspended. Access to the scaffold was given by two iron folding doors in the wall, the pressroom immediately adjoining on the inside, a bridge connecting the one with the other.

Early on Saturday morning people on foot, on horse-back, and in vehicles poured on to the scene in hundreds. The East Lancashire and L. and Y. companies brought in excursionists from the adjoining districts at an all round charge of one shilling a head, and so great was the patronage that, on one train, three engines were required.

When the drop fell there were fully 50,000 persons present.

Immediately below the scaffold there was a barricaded space for the Press and, in this enclosure, there were also a few soldiers, some of the principal witnesses in the case and, strange to say, a number of well dressed women. Seen from within the barriers, the seething, struggling mass of people presented an extraordinary sight, while the smell that arose from them was indescribable.

About half-past eleven a somewhat sensational incident occurred. A dove which had for some time been hovering round the scaffold, settled on the cross beam, and remained until disturbed by the advent of the governor and the Rev. Mr. Marshall. Mr Gibbs was apparently explaining to the priest the construction of the scaffold, and as they re-entered the prison the clergyman took the chain in his hand and very suggestively shrugged his shoulders.

As the time of his execution approached, Gleeson did not abate one whit of the untimely levity which characterised his behaviour since the trial. He passed the Friday walking about his cell whistling, chatting with the Turnkeys on indifferent topics, and in alternately reviling the food supplied to him and the witnesses who appeared against him. He did not retire to rest until three o'clock on the Saturday morning and, when awakened three hours later, he facetiously remarked it would be the last morning he would ever see. The convict had, ever since his sentence, obstinately refused the ministrations of the Church, and it was only between eight and ten o'clock on the morning of his execution that he would enter into devotional exercises.

Owing to a severe attack of illness Calcraft, the executioner, was unable to officiate on the occasion. (This was the reason for the uncertainty of the date of execution the previous week). This was a loss of opportunity to distinguish himself which the executioner afterwards regretted. Indeed, as he explained later, he would have been glad to hang Gleeson Wilson for nothing, and pay his own railway fare.

The day before the execution the services of the York executioner, Howard, were secured. But Howard was a man nearly seventy years of age and, as the sequel will show, quite incompetent to discharge his duties.

At a few minutes before noon Mr. Wilson, the Under-Sheriff, entered the condemned cell to conduct the convict to the pressroom. He was here introduced to the executioner, who showed far more trepidation than did his victim. Howard fumbled about the straps with such indifferent results that the pinioning had to be practically done by the warders. During this operation Wilson sat very quietly, the Priest the while patting him on the shoulder encouragingly. But when the operation was complete, and as he was assisted to his feet, the convict for the first time changed colour and tried to pray.

When the culprit appeared on the scaffold walking between two Priests, who recited the Litany for the dying, it was noticed that he had on his head a white cap. But the cap was not drawn over his face, and those nearest could see that not a muscle of his face moved, and he looked about him with the same jaunty indifference that had characterised his conduct at the trial.

As the convict was placed on the drop, the Priests knelt on either side of him. Wilson did the same, but was immediately raised to his feet by the executioner. Howard, after placing the rope round Wilson's neck, had great difficulty in reaching with the hook the link of the chain, and when this was done the noose was on the left side and had to be moved. The executioner retired, however, without pulling down the white cap, and for a few seconds the crowd had a full view of the culprit as, with his lips moving, he distinctly repeated the responses. At last the clergymen raised their voices as they stepped back, thus heightening the awful situation.

In the midst of the suspense the bolt was drawn and, the cap not covering his face, a fearful picture was presented to the crowd. The drop was a very short one, barely two feet. The distortions of the man's countenance were horrible. Foam came from his lips, the tongue lolled out, and the eyes were starting from his head. The countenance became livid, swollen, and marked with veins that seemed like knotted cords beneath the skin. But the convulsions of the body and the drawing up of the legs lost their spasmodic violence and Howard, reappearing drew down the cap, and mercifully hid a horrible sight from the terror-stricken crowd.

After hanging until one o 'clock the body was taken down by the executioner and two of the warders. As they did so, there were several cries from the crowd for a piece of rope – a request which, of course, was not attended to.

This execution took place in 1849 and is a good example of the many public executions that took place at Kirkdale between 1821, when the prison was built, and the eighteen sixties when executions took place inside the walls. However, nothing improved in either the conditions or humanitarian feelings towards the condemned man at any time during this period, as the next example, of an execution in 1866 will illustrate.

Execution of Thomas Grime, 1866. Executioner – Calcraft.

In January, 1863, James Barton, an engineer in charge of the night-shift at a colliery near Wigan, was missing from his post. An examination of the furnace the following morning ended with the discovery of some human bones and particles of clothing. That these were all that was left of Barton there was no doubt. A series of prolonged investigations terminated in the arraignment of Thomas Grime, at the Summer Assizes, 1866, before Mr. Baron Martin, charged with the wilful murder of Barton.

The chain of evidence against Grime was complete in every link and this, coupled with the charging by Baron Martin, who summed up against the prisoner, left the jury no alternative but to return a verdict of guilty. In passing sentence of death, the judge dwelt strongly on the cowardly and brutal nature of the crime, impressively warning the prisoner that he could look for no mercy on earth.

With the sight of the quadruple execution with which the populace had been favoured in 1863, the authorities had to some extent spoiled the market, a good many people protesting that single executions were scarcely worth going to see.

However, some months having elapsed since even one unfortunate had been put to death in front of Kirkdale, there was a considerable incentive to an increased attendance.

The morning of September 1st broke cold and cheerless, with frequent downfalls of rain; a few persons who, with a view to obtaining a good position, had sought the ground early in the day were soaked to the skin. A few of them had umbrellas, but these offered but small protection to the blinding showers which swept over from the river across the fields; the ground became a perfect morass, an opportunity promptly seized by an enterprising individual who, laying down some long planks, charged threepence a time for a dry foothold. This offer was gladly embraced by some of the more respectable onlookers and for a time all was well. But towards ten o'clock the weather improved somewhat, and the new arrivals coming up in force swept the original holders of the planks fair and square away from their footholds. In consequence, a good many verbal altercations which, at times, threatened to come to blows, ensued. Still, the assemblage, which at noon numbered about 25,000, was as orderly as could be wished, the services of the police who, to the number of 150 or so, were early on the ground, never once being called into requisition.

The erection of the scaffold had commenced on Friday afternoon, but the workmen proceeding at a very leisurely rate, the job was not completed until the Saturday morning. The work was watched with languid interest by the crowd, the bulk of whom bore the appearance of the unemployed clerk class – a fact to be accounted for by the commercial disasters of 1866. That public curiosity would only be partially gratified was plain from the black cloth with which the scaffold was draped, and which would not permit any more view of the culprit than the head to be visible when the drop fell. The authorities had been led to adopt the draping plan from fear of a repetition of the disgusting sights that had been thrust upon the attention of the people at more than one execution.

When the "old hand", Calcraft, had done his work there was no fracture of the vertebral column. His drops averaged two feet and the result, pure strangulation. If the convict had been brought down to a semi-comatose condition, he might lose consciousness with tolerable rapidity. But woe betide him if he stood on the drop with all his facilities about him. He was cast for a long and tough struggle with death in its most appalling form.

There is no coroner's inquest on executed felons and they are rarely seen by anyone, save the gaol surgeon and one or two of the officials. Some awful stories could be told of the appearance of the convicts after death. In one instance the sight was so fearful that even the case-hardened Calcraft, who had come to claim his rope, straps and cap, was not proof against the result of his handiwork, and he left the room to be violently sick outside.

Calcraft arrived late on the Friday night. He was shown to his room in the gaol and, after a hearty supper, he, according to his usual custom, went immediately to bed. So late was he in making his appearance that Grime, who had asked at intervals during the day if the hangman had come, became buoyed up with the kind of feeling that Calcraft would not turn up at all, with the result that the execution would be put off. But the turnkeys assured the prisoner solemnly that Calcraft "never disappointed" and that any hopes of a respite were in vain. The first question asked by Grime when he awoke on Saturday morning was if the executioner had arrived, and the reply in the affirmative sent a distinct shade of sorrow over his by no means bad-looking face.

Since the time of his conviction Grime had displayed a good deal of resignation, and attended earnestly to the ministrations of the Roman Catholic Priest of the Prison.

On the Friday he received visits from some of his relatives, and appeared cheerful, almost happy, in the thought of his impending doom. Pointing to the Agnus suspended from his neck he said that no one wearing that could despair of obtaining salvation adding, in a tone of exultation, that on the day of his execution masses would be said for him "all over the world".

He had from the first refused to talk about the murder, and was greatly offended by any allusion made by the warders to the crime, alleging that he wished to concentrate his thoughts on the future, not talk of the past. The justice of his sentence he tacitly acknowledged, although his statements varied from time to time but, shortly before his execution, he expressed a wish to make a genuine clean breast of it and, having been provided with a slate, did so.

Grime had retired between nine and ten o'clock on the Friday night and, having slept soundly, arose at an early hour and, after having enquired of the executioner, engaged in his devotional exercises. He breakfasted on the usual prison fare; no alteration to the diet having been permitted during his incarceration. He continued to pray with remarkable fervour until a few minutes before noon, when an official entered and intimated he would have to surrender himself into the hands of Calcraft.

From the condemned cell, underneath the prison chapel, Grime was escorted to the Press room. At the sight of the white-bearded, benevolent-looking man who, with his hands on his hips and a collection of straps on either arm, was waiting for his prey, the condemned man seemed as if he would fall, and clung to one of the warders for support. Calcraft stepped forward and, laying his hand on Grime's arm, said soothingly, "I won't hurt you, my boy, and it will soon be over."

Grime braced himself up and submitted patiently to the necessary tightening of the straps and buckles, merely remarking, in a low tone, that "he had often wished to see Calcraft, but never expecting to see him in this way." To the deputy-governor of the gaol, Grime, the pinioning operations being completed, said, "I want to say good-bye to you. Good-bye, my friend, and may God bless you."

While this had been going on inside the prison, the crowd outside had rapidly increased in numbers. There was a good deal of pushing and squeezing and a fair amount of bad language bandied about. But of the rampant ruffianism which had so frequently disgraced the environs of the goal there was nothing observable. By a curious coincidence, neither was there a vestige of a Scripture reader or tract distributor to be seen anywhere in the crowd.

A few minutes before noon the iron door in the wall of the gaol swung open, and public excitement was heightened as one of the officials stepped out and examined the machinery of the drop.

As soon as the pinioning was completed, an informal procession was formed to the scaffold, Grime walking without any support. Precisely at the first stroke of noon from the prison clock, Calcraft stepped onto the scaffold and, having given a nonchalant glance at the sea of faces below and around him, he turned his back upon the crowd and proceeded to adjust Grime, by whom he had been closely followed, upon the drop.

The dying man gave one comprehensive look at the crowd, then closed his eyes, while his lips moved as though in prayer. Calcraft deftly strapped the legs of the murderer who, without the quiver of a single nerve, submitted to that most trying stage of all – the adjustment of the noose.

Calcraft stepped back and placed his hands lightly on his patient's shoulder, as if to steady him. He felt for Grimes right hand and gave it a gentle squeeze, stepping back immediately out of sight. For one brief moment the culprit stood alone before the multitude, over whom a deathlike silence had fallen, while those near the scaffold could see, even through the white cap, his lips moving as though in prayer.

The drop fell with a heavy thud; the body of the murderer disappearing behind the black curtain, and only the vibrations and twitching of the rope told that Thomas Grime was paying tribute to justice for his crime.

The use of a curtain to hide the death-throws of the hanging man, first introduced at Kirkdale, indicates that the Justices and Authorities were becoming concerned over the effect of public hangings on the crowds and within a few years all executions took place out of view of the public.

This sensibility, however, did not improve the actual techniques of hanging, and the Calcraft method of slow strangulation continued behind closed doors, as our next example of execution will demonstrate.

Execution of James Connor, 1873. Executioner – Calcraft

For forty five years Calcraft had been the executioner for England "par excellence". During this period the number of people he put to death must be simply incalculable. For, be it remembered, during a goodly portion of this time many other offences besides wilful murder were capitally punished. Many a morning after a Sessions could mean the stringing up of up to a dozen poor devils, the bulk of whom had sinned, not against life, but property.

With all his experience, Calcraft's techniques could at their best be called clumsy. If the culprit dies easy, so much the better for him. But, if he be at all tenacious of life, his struggles, not infrequently, can be soul-harrowing to witness. Calcraft's penchant for slow strangulation is in his later years much aggravated by his old age and more than once the authorities have suggested he resign his office and leave the work for younger hands. But the old man is a great stickler both for his dignity and his fees. This has resulted in the unfortunate incident reported herewith.

On the 11th August, 1873, James Connor, aged 29, had been to the Cambridge Music Hall, Mill Street, Liverpool. He had there seen a woman named Shears, the wife of a ship's steward and, as the audience was leaving the hall at the conclusion of the performance, he invited her to have a drink. She refused, notwithstanding which he persisted in following her until, at the corner of Mill Street and Jackson Street, he accused her of having some money from him. This she denied. Connor then struck her twice, knocking down the woman, who called "Police!"

James Gaffney who, with a companion named Metcalf, happened to be standing on the other side of the street, crossed over to Connor. Gaffney asked why he had struck the woman. Connor's only reply was to draw a clasp knife and drive it into Gaffney's neck, making as though to strike him with his fist directly afterwards. Metcalf knocked Connor down, but the desperado jumped up immediately and, after stabbing Metcalf, walked away. Gaffney died the next morning in the Southern Hospital, but Metcalf recovered from the effect of his wound, to give evidence at the assizes.

The trial was marked by one or two singular incidents. In the summing up, Mr. Justice Brett told the jury that if Gaffney did not strike Connor, the accused was guilty of wilful murder, but added that if Gaffney even laid his hand on Connor with such an obstructive force as to lead him to imagine that a blow might follow, that, in the eyes of the law, would reduce the crime to manslaughter.

After a short deliberation, the jury asked the judge whether, if no blow was struck – if they honestly thought Connor expected to receive one – they could bring in a verdict of manslaughter? The judge replied that if there was no evidence to prove that Connor had been touched, and no semblance of a blow, then the offence was wilful murder.

After an absence of half an hour, the jury returned to the box and told the judge they were unable to agree on a verdict.

Judge Brett, who during his last colloquy with the jury had been pulling, with ill concealed impatience, his long fawn-coloured whiskers, then addressed them with biting emphasis in every word. After assuring them that if they imagined they could leave the court without delivering a verdict, he was the last person in England to allow them to do so. He pointed out that if any gentleman found himself to be in a large minority, it was his duty to argue out the matter fairly and patiently with his fellows, and not to presume to say that his own opinion was right and that the other jurymen wrong.

The crestfallen jury, who, to put the matter in its mildest form, showed an extraordinary stupidity – for the direction of the judge was so plain a child might have acted upon it – then retired to digest the matter afresh. After another hour's conference they returned a verdict of "Guilty of wilful murder," and Connor was sentenced to death.

The prisoner displayed the utmost callousness during the trial and, when the judge was passing sentence, Connor absolutely smiled at his lordship, remarking in a stage whisper, "You make me laugh!"

From boyhood the condemned man had given himself over to evil courses. Endowed with a lithe active frame, and a good deal of personal strength, he had acquired a considerable local reputation as an amateur boxer and wrestler, devoting to these pursuits the best part of his time.

For a considerable time there was some doubt as to who would act as executioner. Indeed, Calcraft arrived at the gaol at such a late hour on the Sunday night, that some of the officials began to think there would not be any hangman at all.

The representatives of the Press were admitted about 2.30, and, being offered a choice of position from which to view the proceedings, took up their stand in front of the scaffold. At a quarter to eight the prison bell began to toll. As it did so, Calcraft was introduced to the culprit in the small room under the chapel, and began to pinion him. Connor went through the ordeal with wonderful composure, assisting Calcraft to fix the straps in position. As the clock struck eight the procession emerged into the yard.

Connor walked between Father Bronte and Calcraft with a firm jaunty step, paying no attention whatever to the ministrations of the priest.

As he passed the knot of reporters he gave a careless glance at them, and then almost bounded up the few steps leading to the scaffold. He walked straight to the drop and, after casting his eye at the dangling rope, he looked straight to the front, smiling pleasantly and nodding to a couple of warders who stood some distance off. His calmness never deserted him. He bore himself with a reckless bravado, such as even those the most inured to witnessing hangings had never before seen, and of all the groups in the gaol yard the dying man was the only one who was not unnerved.

Calcraft drew the white cap over the condemned man's face, adjusted the rope, strapped the legs, and took his farewell of Connor by touching one of his hands.

41

A moment afterwards the drop fell. As it did so the rope gave way with a rending crack, the broken strands flying up in the air. Connor fell on to a second platform two or three feet below the trap door. His legs and arms being pinioned, he had no means of recovering his balance, and he leaned forward over the edge of the platform, reminding the onlookers with a grotesque awfulness of a puppet in a Punch and Judy show.

Some of the officials immediately attended to the culprit. Two of the warders, with their arms around Connors armpits, tried to lift him out of the hole; but their strength was not equal to the task, and a short stepladder had to be obtained before Connor could be extricated and placed on the upper floor. The trapdoor was then closed and refastened.

Connor, who, directly he fell, gave vent to some exclamations of pain, was placed in a chair. The cap being pulled up from his face, which bore a weary, but not frightened expression.

The mark of the rope was plainly visible round his neck and, where the noose had caught there was a jagged cut, from which blood was issuing. Even the warders were unnerved by the sight, and the eyes of one man filled with tears as Connor, after a series of "Ohs!" of agony, said, "What do you call this? Do you call this murder?" Adding almost immediately, "You should let me go after this. This is surely enough."

Meanwhile, Calcraft, who seemed much distressed, had been wandering about the scaffold in an aimless manner, holding in his hand a piece of broken rope. When one of the officials spoke to him in a reproving whisper, he never answered a word, but gazed with a bewildered expression in the gentleman's face.

Calcraft had a second rope in his bag, but the authorities decided to put their faith in an article to the stoutness of which they could trust. So they sent to the old Press room for one that had done duty before. While everything was being made sure for the next experiment in hanging, Father Bronte tried to attract Connor's attention, stooping down over him and pointing out to him passages in the book of devotions. The poor fellow at first paid no heed to the book, moaning "I have not got over the pain." Then he looked up and responded once or twice, "Lord have mercy upon me." The other rope having been brought, the culprit watched with the utmost concern as Calcraft fastened it securely to the depending hook, remarking, "I stood it like a brick the first time."

Observing that Calcraft was ready, Connor got up from the chair unassisted, and placed himself on the drop. His arms being only pinioned at the elbow he stooped his head so he might draw the cap over his face himself, and assisted Calcraft in placing the noose round his neck. Again Calcraft drew the bolt.

For a moment or two the tortured man seemed lifeless. Then began the dreadful twitching of the body and lower limbs to tell how much he suffered. And little wonder when it is considered that the length of the second drop was only eight inches ... Connor died hard! The bolt was pulled out the first time at 8.02, the second time at 8.10. So the judicial slaughter lasted over eight minutes!

No one could say who was to blame for this awful blundering. Calcraft, for some years had brought his own ropes, although they were at one time supplied by the gaol authorities. The hangman's first remark was, "I could have staked my life on that rope." He then denied that the rope broke at all, alleging the noose had become unfastened. But one of the warders who had the noose part of the rope intact, disposed of this assertion easily.

Calcraft, when examined at an inquest, deposed he was 73 years of age, and had acted as executioner since 1828. He said that the rope, which measured a little over half an inch in diameter, was quite new, had never been used before, and had been tested with a weight of 3 cwt. over a fall of three feet.

The authorities decided to dispense with the services of Calcraft for the future.

CHAPTER SEVEN

For two years, after the "retirement" of Calcraft, executions at Kirkdale prison were carried out by a strange man. He was a real mystery man, known as Mr. Anderson. He didn't socialise with anyone, even the prison staff, and all sorts of rumours were spread about Liverpool and the stories, in their telling, gathered embellishment as to who he was and where he came from. In fact, he was a farmer from Deeside and, in the past, had assisted Calcraft in several executions. Although his career was brief he was relatively efficient, but he had a tremendous impact on people due to his manner and appearance, putting the fear of God into many of the lawless section of the people of Liverpool.

The next report gives a very good description, not only of Mr. Anderson's work, but also of the atmosphere in the yard at the time of execution.

Execution of Corrigan, 1873. Executioner – Anderson/nee Evans

On Saturday November 1st, Thomas Corrigan returned to his home at No. 36, Chisenhale Street, considerably the worse for drink, went beserk and having assaulted several members of his family and neighbours, he struck and jumped on his Mother, who died. He was arraigned at the winter assizes in 1873, the defence being undertaken by a Mr. Thurlow, who adopted the line that Corrigan had committed the crime while labouring under a fit of the "D.T.s" and this was in itself sufficient to reduce the offence to one of manslaughter. Corrigan was, however, convicted of murder, and the judge, in passing sentence, remarked upon the enormity of the crime he had committed in taking away the life of one he was bound by all laws, human and divine, to love and cherish.

As his days on earth shortened Corrigan applied himself with much earnestness to the ministrations of Father Bronte and, on the Saturday before his execution, he was visited by his father, the leave taking between them being of a most affecting character. The old man clung to his son with a fondness he had never before exhibited, Corrigan showing a tenderness and love it was thought his brutal nature was incapable of.

The morning of the execution broke drear and cold. The moon was shining brightly when those whose duty it was to be present left their homes for the prison. An Inspector and a few constables on duty before the gates of Kirkdale had a very easy task, no one putting in an appearance to break the monotony of their patrol until the cabs bringing the reporters drove up.

At eight o'clock there was a pale grey dawn, through which, those who had been conducted into the prison to witness the fearful scene, could distinguish the outline of the gallows. Depending from the centre of the cross-beam was the hangmans hook, the link of short chain and the rope, with which the last scene of the drama would be enacted, being twisted carelessly around it, while close to the scaffold a gas lamp shed its dim rays on the scene, throwing long shadows into the morning mist.

Corrigan was a stoutly-built young man and, in order to avoid a repetition of the catastrophe at Connor's execution, a considerably thicker rope had been provided. The prison bell began to toll a few minutes before eight o'clock and, at this signal, those present took up their positions in front of the gallows. To avoid the painful walk across the gaol yard, Corrigan had been removed at about seven o'clock and placed in a storeroom a few feet from the scaffold steps.

On the previous Sunday Corrigan had attended service in the Roman Catholic chapel in the prison. At this time, at the request of the culprit, Father Bronte had used the sad epoch in his life to point out a moral to the other prisoners, beseeching them to amend the error of their ways and, as a first step thereto, to take the temperance pledge.

Corrigan had slept until half past five, when he arose. A little before seven o'clock he partook of a slight breakfast, having been taken to the storeroom near the scaffold. He was perfectly resigned and, even when, just as the prison bell began to toll away the last minutes of his earthly career, the executioner entered the room and proceeded to pinion him, he did not betray the slightest emotion.

No one was sure who was to perform the last office of the law. The authorities had rejected Calcraft after his last fiasco, and the old man, whose constitution was deteriorating after the wear and tear of years of public service, was unable to move. His place was filled by a man whose name was said to be Anderson. He was a middle sized man, closely shaven, with very sharp features, and keen, deep set eyes. He was immaculately dressed in all black, and throughout the proceedings wore a black skull cap. He pinioned his victim with great rapidity, at the same time with the utmost consideration.

Shortly after the clock struck eight the procession emerged from the room and ascended the steps of the scaffold. The prisoner, pinioned as he was, walked unaided, Father Bronte at his side with his hand under the culprit's elbow, a position which the reverend gentlemen kept until Corrigan was on the drop. Corrigan was a stoutly-built youth of medium height. He had a bull neck and a heavy jowl, while his hair, so red as to be almost brilliant scarlet, grew down almost to his eyebrows. Although he walked firmly, his naturally florid complexion had given way to an ashen pallor. When Anderson's long fingers touched the back of his neck, while adjusting the noose, Corrigan give a convulsive shudder, which was almost a jump. The executioner did his work with wonderful celerity. He had pinioned the prisoner's legs, adjusted the rope, and pulled the white cap over his eyes in less time than it takes to write about it. Then with the lever in his hand he waited a second and as soon as Corrigan was in the act of uttering one of the responses the bolt was pulled, and the murderer remained suspended.

There was a slight struggle or two after Corrigon fell, but he appeared to die easy, although after his execution, when the officials had left the scaffold, a quiver of the limbs told that life had not been extinguished at once, but was gradually ebbing away.

After the body had hung for an hour, the executioner, two warders, and a couple of prisoners in gaol clothes, took the body off the hook and removed it to the pinioning room, where they placed it on a board. On pulling up he cap the face appeared perfectly placid, only the mark of the rope telling of the violence of his death.

At the inquest, the Governor, upon being asked by whom the execution had been performed, had to profess his ignorance, saying the man had assisted previously and that his letters were addressed "A.B.C." or something of the sort.

Meanwhile, the male prisoners had been going round the yard in circles, while two of their number were disjointing the machine of justice, and, in a couple of hours, the only trace of the judicial avenging of the Chisenhale Street murder is a slightly raised mound in the prison "churchyard."

CHAPTER EIGHT

Mr Anderson continued to work at Kirkdale until 1875 before retiring into anonymity, leaving the scene with as little notice as when he arrived to perform his first legal function. He left behind him a reputation and a sensation of fear that few men have ever achieved in influencing the outlook of Liverpool people. "Mr Anderson will get you" became a constant warning given by parents to misbehaving children, and nearly all of them grew up believing it.

His final job was to attend to justice on a well known group of young men who had terrorised the centre of Liverpool with their rowdy behaviour in 1874. With them he hung another criminal for an entirely unrelated crime, illustrating that in the nineteenth century, one couldn't even achieve privacy for one's own execution. The following report gives a description of a multiple hanging.

Execution of Mullen, McCrave & Worthington, 1875. Executioner – Anderson

On August Bank Holiday, 1874, Robert Morgan, a 26 year old working man, was returning with his wife and brother from a trip to New Ferry. They were quietly making their way home along Tithebarn Street, Morgan being next to the wall, his wife in the centre and his brother on the outside.

At the corner of Milk Street, Campbell, Mullen, McCrave with other young men, who liked to call themselves "The High Rip Gang", were standing in front of a public house. As the Morgans were passing, McCrave said to the husband "Give us six pence for ale." Morgan replied to the effect that if people wanted beer money they should work for it. McCrave then struck him under the left ear, knocking him into the roadway. Morgan never spoke again. McCrave was joined by Mullen and Campbell, the trio proceeding to treat their victim's body as if it were a football, kicking him across the roadway, a distance of forty feet. Mrs Morgan threw herself on her husband to shield him from further outrage, but was pulled off and brutally kicked by Campbell.

It speaks volumes for the dastardly nature of the surroundings, that this outrage was witnessed by a large crowd, who not only declined to interfere, but actually cheered on and encouraged the roughs in their brutality. Morgan's brother had behaved with praiseworthy pluck, having fought with the young men all the time, but it was not until the arrival of the police, heralded by the customary "Eck!" "Eck!" that the prolonged assault terminated, and the ruffians made off.

McCrave was captured the same evening. Mullen was taken the next day, having stowed away on board a ship. Campbell was taken a few days later. After the trial and sentence of death of the three boys, for they were little more, being of seventeen years of age, with Mullen looking only fifteen, strong efforts were made by their families and friends to secure their reprieve.

To the credit of the Home Secretary be it said, the petition was only listened to in the case of Campbell who, chiefly on account of his previous good character, had his sentence commuted to penal servitude for life. However, with the exception of the few so opposed to capital punishment they would sue for the reprieve of a Fisk or a Peace, it is satisfactory to add that public opinion ran high against the young villains. As it was, a side-wind proposal, that McCrave and his companions should be flogged to death was cordially endorsed by the people.

Pending their execution Mullen and McCrave came out in very different colours, the latter whose evil career had earned for him the soubriquet of "Holy Fly," showed the white feather right through the piece, having the greatest fear of death and a nameless dread of the executioner. On the other hand Mullen, who was only seventeen years of age, maintained from first to last a strong indifference which nothing could move. His sole remark to the executioner, as the cap was being pulled over his face, "Snap me off quick!" was a good index to his stubborn, relentless character.

At the same winter assizes a flatman, named Worthington, was sentenced to death. It was a simple case of wife murder, brutal, but ordinary, the victim being in bad health at the time. As Worthington pathetically remarked "It is a shame to hang a man for killing a woman who was already half dead."

The morning of January 3rd, 1875, broke cold, foggy and miserable.

The spell of frost, which had reached its climax on New Years Eve, still kept its hold on the ground and locomotion near the prison was attended with a good deal of danger to limb, if not to life.

Dark and dreary, beyond expression, looked the generally gloomy yard of Kirkdale, as the few whose duty it was to be present picked their way to the position assigned to them. Dimly looming through the fog could be seen the misty outline of the gibbet, with its three short links of chain, attached to which, and carefully coiled up, were three substantial looking ropes.

At five minutes to eight the fog became so thick that it was doubtful whether any part of the proceedings would be visible to the reporters. A warder came out and lighted a lamp near the steps to the gallows, while a faint light glimmering from the pinioning room told that the preliminary operations were already in progress.

As the prison clock was about to strike eight, the death bell which, for a quarter of an hour had been mournfully tolling, rang out a few sharp strokes. As it did the procession, headed by the chief warder, emerged from the prison buildings. Worthington and the executioner walked side by side. Then came Mullen, followed by McCrave, and the Rev. Father Bronte, who recited the offices for the dead, the acting under-sheriff, the governor of the gaol and some wardens bringing up the rear.

Worthington, who walked with an unsteady gait, seemed to feel his position acutely. Mullen maintained a stoic impassibility, but McCrave was simply terror stricken and, on coming in sight of the scaffold, looked as if about to faint. At the steps a halt was made. The executioner, Mr Anderson, who, in a black overcoat, from the breast pocket of which peeped a white cambric handkerchief, took Worthington by the arm, placing him in position under the beam. As he pulled the white cap over his face and adjusted the rope, the culprit, who held in his hand a white pocket handkerchief, fervently repeated the responses. Mullen, who was then brought up, showed no signs of fear, submitting quietly to the attentions of the hangman. McCrave looked fearsomely up at the rope and when the noose was put around his neck shivered like an aspen leaf, repeating in a tremulous voice, "Lord be merciful to me!" "Christ be merciful to me a sinner!" The executioner then fastened the legs of each culprit with a strap, and then – the whole operation having taken but a few seconds – he shook hands with the men in turn. As he did so the chaplain and officials left the scaffold. During this trying period Worthington repeated the responses, Mullen stood silently with his hands clasped, with McCrave asking frantically to be saved.

As the trap fell, a loud "Oh!" burst from one of the culprits, to be cut short by the silence of death. The bodies swayed slightly, but the hangman steadied them with his hands on their shoulders, and they all came to a standstill in the same position, with the head hanging over the left shoulder.

There was not the slightest struggle, which, considering the drop was only two and a half feet, speaks volumes for the skill of the executioner, who is said to have a wide knowledge of surgery.

This was "Mr Andersons" last execution. His "de haut en bas" treatment of prison officials had told against him and he had received an intimation that his services would not be required again.

Marwood took over the duties of executioner at Kirkdale in 1875 and continued for the next seven years. He was a gentleman who came from Horncastle and, being of a sociable nature, compared to the remote, arrogant and mysterious Mr Anderson, he was immediately "accepted" by both the officials at the prison and the ordinary people of Liverpool, who were always endeavouring to have a joke at his expense.

He was a clever man, who considered his work to be an art form, constantly developing techniques of execution which were carried on long after his retirement. He must be especially remembered for his development of "the long drop", which did so much to reduce the suffering of the condemned man.

The next example of execution detailed here, was the first execution Marwood attended to at Kirkdale, although strangely, it wasn't a local crime, but a case that had been remitted over from Manchester to Liverpool Assizes.

Execution of Alfred Thomas Heap, 1875. Executioner – Marwood

Alfred Thomas Heap called himself a surgeon, but had no diploma or any qualification whatever to call himself a medical man. He had a herbalist's shop in Hyde Road and would have appeared to have obtained considerable vogue by the prescription of cheap and harmless herbal remedies for simple ailments. However, his greatest reputation was for dealing with unwanted pregnancies.

Mary McKivett was a single woman who kept a confectioner's shop not far from Heap's place of business. Finding herself pregnant – it was alleged through an uncle – in the spring of 1875, she borrowed a sovereign to cover his fees, and set out accompanied by her mother. They parted some distance from Heap's shop and, when the latter next saw her daughter, the operation had been performed, which resulted in the death of the unfortunate girl.

The arraignment was at the Spring Assizes, 1875, before Mr. Baron Pollock. Heap was ably defended by Mr Foard, who argued that the offence was, if anything, manslaughter; but the jury, on the evidence available, had no alternative but to find him guilty of wilful murder. This verdict, however, they coupled with a recommendation to mercy, and there is little doubt that Heap would have been reprieved had there not been recorded against him a prior sentence of five years penal servitude, also for procuring abortion.

Heap showed himself a very tractable prisoner, paying the greatest attention to the ministrations of the gaol chaplain. During the last week of his life he prepared a long statement in writing, having reference to the details of his crime. This he desired might be published, so the public might have an opportunity of knowing he was not so black as he was supposed to be. Mr. Piggot, the prison chaplain, preached the condemned sermon on the Sunday before the execution from the text "The terrors of death have fallen on me." Which must have made very cheerful listening for all the prisoners present, as well as the condemned man. As usual, in such sermons, Mr. Piggot also managed to get in loads of references to the devil and the evils of drink.

Marwood arrived on the Saturday evening, and took up his quarters at the Sessions House Hotel. It was on this occasion that Calcraft and Mr. Anderson, the previous executioners, got together with Marwood, presumably to "talk shop". Friends of the group, who had joined them, recorded that their sole subject of conversation was on method and technique. This was to be expected as they all knew one another, having assisted each other at various times in the past. Later in the evening Marwood went with an old friend from Liverpool who insisted on taking him down town and showing him Liverpool by night. His friend took him to several well-known hostelries, where the advent of Marwood – for he was introduced very freely to a lot of people – created a sensation. The couple were followed along Lime Street by a large crowd, and the attentions of their admirers became at length so pointed, that they had to seek asylum in a four wheeler.

Marwood was introduced to his patient about twenty minutes to eight, and found him engaged in devotional exercises with the chaplain. Heap stepped towards the executioner, but Marwood, looking at his watch, coolly remarked, "Don't hurry yourself, sir. My job won't take five minutes, and it's no good your being strapped up before you are obliged to be." While Heap and the chaplain knelt side by side, he proceeded to open his bag and methodically select his straps, first of all placing the white cap in his pocket.

At six minutes to eight he again looked at his watch, and tapped Heap on the shoulder. The wretched man, who knew the full strength of the signal, rose to his feet and, while the chaplain continued to intone the prayers, raised his hands above his head to admit Marwood passing the broad halter belt around his waist.

The morning was a glorious one, the sun shining with a warmth more suggestive of June than of April. By half past seven, groups of persons, mostly of the labouring class, began to collect round and about the gaol, mostly in the vicinity of the north-west angle of the prison, where the public executions used to be carried out, and where, even to this day, the comparative newness of some of the bricks shows the locality of the great iron doors which led from the gaol to the scaffold. Several policemen were on duty at the entrance to the gaol, where nearly a score of reporters were awaiting admission. At a quarter to eight, the outer wicket was unbarred, giving entrance to the pressmen who, after a brief delay before the second door, crossed the yard to the front of the scaffold. All was quiet and the solemn silence only broken by the mournful tolling of the death bell.

The bright sun gave to the gallows, with its black beam and sombre draping, a more dismal appearance than on a dull morning. Coiled up on the beam was the rope which, it was noticed, was of more than usual length and thickness. The colour was a convincing proof that it was a virgin rope, and a closer examination led to the supposition that it had been manufactured expressly for the horrible job, the strands not being twisted too tightly, so there might be no fear of snapping at the sudden jerk.

A few moments before eight the procession passed out of the reception room, the chaplain, reading the Litany for the dying, walked on the right hand of the culprit, who was followed by two warders, Marwood coming next. The few steps leading to the scaffold were soon ascended and the doomed man placed himself under the cross beam, casting his eyes upwards as Marwood

53

adjusted him to the position he required. As Heap stood on the drop he looked a well formed man, tall, slender, and of what might be called smart build. He was attired in the same clothes he had worn at his trial, a rather dingy suit of black. The executioner quickly strapped his legs, placed the white cap over the face, and then adjusted the rope, taking particular care to have the knot in a certain position. This appeared to be the work of a moment or two.

As the clock gave the first stroke of eight, Marwood withdrew from the condemned man, took hold of the handle of the lever which governs the bolt, and there was a slight pause. With his hand on the lever Marwood looked directly at the chaplain as an intimation that all was ready. The chaplain, in a loud voice, cried "Lord Jesus, receive the soul of Alfred Thomas Heap." The prisoner just audibly replied, "Receive my soul." and, before the clock had finished the eighth stroke, the bolt was drawn and the unfortunate man launched into eternity.

Death appeared to be instantaneous, the length of the drop being five and a half feet. The thud of the trapdoor was extremely loud and could be distinctly heard by persons outside the gaol. After the drop had fallen the body never moved, neither was there any motion of the limbs. The tremors which were obvious at previous executions to pass through the body were absent and there was no swaying of the rope. Possibly the latter was due to a plank which was so placed that the front of the man's legs rested against it after the fall, so the body was prevented from swinging round. A close inspection showed a movement of the white cap just over the mouth, as though occasioned by the ebbing breath. The rope was drawn tightly round the neck, and the verteral column appeared to be effectually severed. After hanging an hour the body was cut down and later in the day buried within the prison.

The Liverpool Summer Assizes of 1875 was a trying time for Mr. Justice Archibald who presided on the Crown side, for he sentenced no less than seven to death in different trials. No wonder it became known as "The Black Assize". All the condemned were placed in Kirkdale and although some were reprieved, Marwood was kept busy, developing and improving the technique of execution by the long drop, as the following report of a double execution shows. These, once again were unrelated cases, one being a popular Liverpool publican and the other an American seaman.

At the time the murder was committed, William Baker managed the Railway Vaults at the corner of Houghton Street and Williamson Square. At some period of his career he seems to have made the acquaintance of the murdered man, Charles Langan but, according to evidence offered at the trial, the relations between the parties had been for some time considerably strained.

Baker spent the evening of July 10th 1875, at a public house in Scotland Road. In company with three other men he left about eleven o'clock, and went towards his own place in Williamson Square. After calling at several refreshment houses on the way home, they directed their steps towards an illicit drinking house in Back Bridport Street, but were refused admission by the landlord. At the time they called, Langan and some of his friends were on the point of leaving the house; the result being they followed the Baker party up Back Bridport Street, in the direction of London Road. Opposite the Swan Inn, Baker called out to Langan, who crossed over to him, when some words ensued. Immediately on this, there seems no doubt that Baker pulled out a revolver and shot Langan. He was removed to the Royal Infirmary where life was found to be extinct.

At the Summer Assizes, Baker was arraigned before Mr. Justice Archibald and, after a patient hearing which lasted the whole day, convicted and sentenced to death. The verdict was accompanied by a recommendation to mercy, resulting from a compromise among the jury, one of whom was in favour of reducing the crime to manslaughter. Baker's defence was conducted by Mr. Pope, who made a masterly appeal to the jury on behalf of his client.

During the trying ordeal of the day Baker bore himself wonderfully well. With his right hand clasping the rail of the dock, he listened with an unmoved expression to the sentence of death.

Never, in the recollection of officials, had so much public interest been displayed in any case as in the trial of Baker. From an early hour in the morning until after the verdict was made known, the steps and platform in front of St. George's Hall were packed by an excited throng, who used all kinds of subterfuges to obtain admission to the building.

Extraordinary efforts were made to secure the reprieve of the condemned man. One petition to the Home Secretary was signed by "eleven of the jury" and ten members of the Town Council, including Messrs. Woodruffe, R. C. Gardner, and Robertson Gladstone. The terms of the petition, containing as it did some serious reflections upon the character of the deceased man, called forth an indignant letter of refutation, signed by his brother on behalf of the Langan family, the following clause of which is worth preserving "Our brother may not have led a blameless life, but we respectfully submit his life is quite as valuable as that of the person who took it."

For the other man, who suffered the extreme penalty, there was a good deal of well deserved pity. His name was Edward Cooper, his crime the murder on the high seas of the boatswain of the ship on which he was a seaman. Cooper shot the man under circumstances of great provocation, and there is no doubt that if he had friends to take up his cause, he would have been reprieved. Unfortunately he stood alone, his only relative being his mother living in New Orleans. Of death he had no fear whatever, his only desire being that he should be shot instead of hung. Cooper had always borne an irreproachable character, and had sailed in the same employ for a number of years.

He was a remarkably fine looking man, standing fully six feet high and of a corresponding build, with a crisp curling beard and a frank open expression. Professing himself to be a Roman Catholic, he received the earnest care of the Rev. Father Bronte, to whose ministrations he paid the most devout attention.

The prison officials found Cooper unusually tractable and, to one who had him under his care during the latter part of his incarceration, I am indebted for the following particulars. Baker soon after his conviction fell into a state of semi-collapse, to remove which, the prison doctor ordered him a liberal diet. This he would hardly touch. Cooper's appetite, however, like his spirits, was unimpaired, so much so that the prison diet was all too meagre for him. The attendant, therefore, used to slip across to Baker's cell and bring over the almost untouched food to his charge, who would eat it heartily, and with much thankfulness.

Cooper wore at his trial a handsome shirt, a mixture of silk and cotton, of a very peculiar pattern. Of this article he was very proud. Shortly after his conviction, this shirt was taken from him, the authorities telling him it was to be washed. Cooper never saw his shirt again. It was the only bit of personal property he had and time after time he asked for it – but asked in vain. The excuse was that although washed it had not yet been ironed, and it was only on the way to the scaffold that he fully realised he was not to have his shirt again. His plaintive remark "They might have let me be hung in it." stayed in the memory of those accompanying him.

As the day of execution approached, public interest in the London Road tragedy deepened considerably and, on the Sunday night before the curtain fell on the last act, crowds of people collected outside the closed doors of the Rainbow, as the public house was nicknamed and, while they talked over the matter, glanced curiously up at the closed blinds.

Baker, who during his confinement wept frequently and bitterly, did not go to bed until one on the Monday morning, when his slumbers were fitful and troubled. Cooper slept soundly and ate a tolerably hearty breakfast; chatting away the while unconcernedly to his attendants.

The morning of the execution found Kirkdale Gaol once again totally enveloped in a heavy mist. Between seven and eight o'clock the men were removed from their cells to the reception room near the foot of the scaffold, where they were pinioned by Marwood. Pending the hour of execution, those whose duty it was to be present, together with members of the Press, had an opportunity of inspecting the scaffold.

Two short links of chain depended from the cross beam, and to these were attached two carefully coiled up ropes. These were considerably longer than those which had been used before at Kirkdale. It was noticed that the one on the left side was much thicker than the other, and looked more coarsely spun. A good length of the thinner rope was caught up and looped round the chain, as if Marwood had intended to give Baker a much longer drop than he eventually did. The ordinary tied noose of previous hangings had been replaced by a brass-lined eyelet through which the rope ran. Above this was a stout leather washer, to prevent the noose, once adjusted, slipping from its position.

Just before eight o'clock, again accompanied by the sound of the death bell, which could be heard for miles around, the doors of the reception room were thrown open, and the voices of the Rev. Father Bronte and the Rev. Mr. Pigott could be heard intoning their different versions of the final ministrations. The head warden appeared followed by Cooper with a warden by his side, Father Bronte following. Cooper, who looked resigned but unconcerned, walked as firmly as though treading the deck of a vessel at sea and, on reaching the platform, placed himself firmly on the drop, stamping his foot as if to test the solidity of the structure. The latter part of the procession hung some distance behind, probably owing to the weakness of Baker who came into view in a pitiable condition, supported by a warder. His upturned face was deathly pale, and his head hung back, swaying from side to side. Following Baker came Mr. Pigott, then Marwood, the Governor and other officials bringing up the rear.

As Marwood was strapping his legs, Cooper said in a strong clear voice, "All I can say is that I have not got justice." And very few people thought he had! Marwood got through his work with wonderful celerity. He strapped the men's legs, pulled down the caps, and adjusted the ropes like a streak of lightning. Then, without a seconds pause, he touched the lever, and the doors fell with a thunderous crash, which could be heard far from the prison perimeter. The drop was six feet, three inches, and death must have been instantaneous. No motion whatever being detected in the bodies after the bolt was drawn. Immediately the drop fell, Father Bronte walked off the scaffold, but Mr. Pigott remained kneeling for a few moments over Baker's body, in prayer.

The last to leave the scaffold was Marwood who, when all had left, very composedly stood on the brink of the abyss, and drawing a red handkerchief from his pocket, cooly wiped his face as he contemplated the bodies below him. Then, assured that his task had been satisfactorily accomplished, he walked quietly away, and was lost from view in a room near the prison entrance.

CHAPTER NINE

Events in the daily life of the prison were recorded by the Governor in his diary. This was, in the main, a report on his findings during his daily round of inspection, which incorporated his opinion on the health of the prisoners, including those who could be terminally ill. Punishments awarded, not only to the prisoners, but to the staff, (who often had to be disciplined, usually because of the effects of alcohol). He also recorded his personal opinions of prisoners, and the ultimate affects of punishment upon their behaviour.

The main administrative records of the prison, however, were not kept by the Governor, but by the prison Chaplain. He performed many duties as well as his religious functions and was paid a relatively high salary, receiving only £100 less than the Governor and considerably more than the prison doctor and matron. He was the main administrator of the prison, probably because of his better background and the education he had received. Usually he was only known for accompanying the condemned to the gallows and for Sunday services and sermons. But he used to keep records of every possible event and fact. The yearly Chaplains reports prove to be the most informative on the prison population.

The Chaplain's job was an extremely lucrative sinecure, receiving a good salary and a house, second in grandeur to the Governor's residence.

All the Chaplains appointed to Kirkdale, throughout its existence, seem to have been obsessed with the "evils of drink", preaching on the subject at every opportunity, week in week out, and many a poor devil went to his death on the gallows hearing how alcohol caused his downfall. As it was too late to do anything about it and they were fed-up with the same lecture, they were probably glad to go.

However, allowing for a certain amount of bias in the reports, they were a very good record of the types of convict and their social background. The Chaplain also seems to have been the only approachable person the prisoners could talk to. They also took it upon themselves to act as, what nowadays would be called, a probation officer, following up the careers of released convicts, and seeming to be genuinely pleased when they achieved relative respectability. Many released convicts actually wrote (or had someone write for them) letters of thanks and appreciation.

The Chaplain was always High Church of England, with visiting Priests of other denominations making regular calls and officiating at functions (such as executions) involving their own followers.

CHAPTER TEN

In the Eighteen-Nineties, the use of the County Gaol at Kirkdale had been supplanted by the new Walton Gaol. The formation of a Prisons Department, Governed by Commissioners, by an Act of Parliament in 1877, was beginning to have an effect, with improved prison buildings being erected throughout the Country. Kirkdale, as a County Gaol, was redundant to requirements.

The last report on Kirkdale Prison to the Commissioners of Prisons, for the Year ended 31st March 1892, reads as follows:-

"KIRKDALE PRISON"

There have been no men available for 1st class hard labour during the past year. Labour in the 2nd class consisted of mat and rug making, weaving handkerchiefs, picking oakum, etc ...

The conduct of the officers has been very good.

The dietaries have been sound and wholesome, and the contractors' supplies good and according to contract.

The prisoners generally have behaved well.

There had been a large decrease in the population of this prison during the past four years. In 1889 the daily average was 441, but in 1890 it fell to297, and in 1890 to 219, whilst the number for the past year was only 51. The number of committals was 181, of these 178 were debtors and 1st class misdemeanants. Only 92 prisoners were transferred from Liverpool Prison.

The prison was occupied from 1st April 1891 to 16th February 1892, when the last two prisoners in custody were transfered to Liverpool Prison.

The health of the prisoners was very well maintained, there were no deaths nor any prisoner pardoned on mental grounds; although influenza was prevalent in the neighbourhood, there was perfect freedom from it in the prison, and the majority of the cases of sickness was not of a serious character.

As a matter of interest, the only people who expressed regret at leaving Kirkdale Prison, were the last two prisoners mentioned in the report. They were "old retainers". Two long term convicts, whose main job in the past was to look after the chapel gardens and to dig graves for the burial of executed prisoners.

A hundred years have now passed since the death bell tolled over the prison, its solemn message ringing out over the River Mersey. The sombre building has gone, replaced by a recreation ground, where the sound of children playing has replaced the screams of the condemned and the mad.

People go about their normal way of life in a close knit residential area. But! ... and anyone who lives in the area will tell you. Anyone walking in the recreation ground at night or in the mists of the Mersey "knows" there is something different about the place ... Do hands reach up from the cold earth searching for peace and understanding?

Why did I record these historical facts? I am not too sure. I was born and raised next to the prison. My own children played on the recreation ground.

But, most of all, I think it is because my own Grandmother, who raised me, was the last Matron of the prison and I owe a debt to the memory of the many people who passed through the gates.

Horner W.   Liverpool Record Office
   Chaplain at Kirkdale
   Report 1825
   Chaplain at Kirkdale   Liverpool Record Office.
   Reports, various 1848+
Liverpool Courier. Reports 1837+
Liverpool Review. Report 1888+   Liverpool Record Office.
Map of Kirkdale 1840.   Liverpool Record Office.
Broadsheets.   Liverpool Record Office.
Porcupine. Reports (Publication) 1866/1870 Liverpool Record Office.
The Pamphleteer XXIII. 1824   British Library.
Lancashire County Salaries Records   Lancashire Records Office,
                                                 Preston.

Calendars of Crown Prisoners (QJC)   Lancashire Records Office,
                                                 Preston.

Reports by Governors, Chaplains and   Lancashire Records Office,
   Surgeons, 1823-1867   Preston.
Abstract of Returns made by Overseers   Lancashire Records Office,
   of the Poor   Preston.
Lancaster Prison Records   Lancashire Records Office,
   1805/21 (QJC/1)1   Preston.
Kirkdale Records 1821-1834 (QJC/2)   Lancashire Records Office,
                                                 Preston.

Report (15th) of the Commissioners   Prison Service Library,
   of Prisons (1892)   Wakefield.
Coroners' Inquisitions (PL25/285-95)   Public Record Office, London.
Assize Rolls. Lancashire (PL25)(All)   Public Record Office, London.
Assize Indictments, Lancashire (PL26/27)   Public Record Office, London.
Correspondence and Papers on   Public Record Office, London.
   Disturbances (1812-1855) (HO40)
Assizes & Q.S. Liverpool 1840-63   Public Record Office, London.
   (PCOM2/319-328)
Liverpool Borough Sessions 1812-1843   Public Record Office, London.
   (PCOM2/330-341)

Journals and Letter Book   Public Record Office, London.
   Lancashire Gaolers (PCOM2/442-448)

Reports of Inspectors of Prisons   Public Record Office, London.
   Digest of Returns

Chesterton. "Revelations of Prison Life"
   London 1856.

Howard. "State of the Prisons" 3rd Edition.
   London 1774-1782.

Baly. "Comparative Death Rates in
   Lancashire Prisons" 1838-42.